DECISIONS MADE SIMPLE

A QUICK GUIDE TO GUIDANCE

TIM CHESTER

EP Books (Evangelical Press), Registered Office: 140 Coniscliffe Road, Darlington, Co Durham DL3 7RT

admin@epbooks.org www.epbooks.org

EP Books are distributed in the USA by:

JPL Books, 3883 Linden Ave. S.E., Wyoming, MI 49548

order@jplbooks.com www.jplbooks.com

British Library Cataloguing in Publication Data available

Print ISBN 978-1-78397-261-6

eBook ISBN 978-1-78397-262-3

CONTENTS

DECISION-MAKING AND THE WILL OF GOD

Have you ever had to make a decision? Of course you have. We make decisions every day. Each morning we decide what to wear, maybe our blue top or our red top, whether to have cornflakes or toast (or both), whether to take one road or another to work, how to respond to an email or a colleague's request. And so on.

Most of the time we make these decisions without much thought. But there are some decisions we agonise over and which fill us with angst. Who to marry? Which church to join? Where to live? What job to do? To stay or go?

So this is a vital topic for Christians. We want to make decisions that honour Christ and that conform to God's will. That can add to the angst. Like everyone else we're trying to figure out what *we* want, but Christians are also trying to figure out what *God* wants.

Not only is it more of a challenge for Christians; it's more of a challenge in our day. We make far more significant decisions that most people have in the past. Two or three generations ago where you lived and what you did was largely determined by your parents. There was little social or geographic mobility. Most people did the job their father or mother had done. You lived in the community in which you were born. Even who you married might be largely determined by your family.

Today life is much more fluid. We have a far greater capacity to choose what we do, where we live, who we love and even who we are. This is a great blessing. But it does come with increased angst. In the past your identity was largely given to you. Today, who we are is increasingly the product of the choices we make. So those choices carry extra weight because our identity is at stake.

So decision-making is relevant to all of us, every day of our lives, and particularly when we have big choices to make—the kind of choices that alter the course of our lives.

The will of God

The problem is that people often have a view of guidance that, while it sounds very spiritual, does not reflect the teaching of Scripture. And this faulty view makes decision-making even more angst-ridden. Perhaps you've heard people say things like:

- 'I'm asking God to reveal to me whether I should take this job.'
- 'We shouldn't just ask God to bless *our* plans—we should ask him to show us *his* plans.'
- 'Make sure you don't miss God's will for your life.'
- 'I'm seeking God's will.'

Statements like these sound so spiritual and often they're driven by a good desire to obey God. But their premise is not biblical. They assume God has a specific and unique plan for the life of each Christian. They assume God has chosen a partner, a job, a ministry for you, and your job is to discover God's will so you can act upon it. And, by the way, if you get it wrong, things will go badly. No wonder we get anxious!

And then things gets worse because God doesn't always seem to make his will crystal clear. So some people look for signs or special words. Other people try to read God's will from circumstances or a sense of peace in their hearts. No wonder some Christians are left in a state of confusion or even paralysis. They're so concerned not to step out of God's will that they hesitate ever to step forward.

So let me state this clearly: while God sometimes intervenes to guide his people, *a specific divine direction for your life is not the norm* in the Bible. I realise it's often a deeply held assumption. People read it into all sorts of Bible verses. But it's not taught in God's word.

Let's bring some biblical clarity by looking at how the word of God talks about the will of God. It does so in two ways—God's sovereign will and his moral will. But it doesn't speak of God's will in three ways—it doesn't speak in terms of a person-specific will.

God's sovereign will

First, the Bible talks about God's sovereign will. Everything that happens, happens because God decides that it should happen. Nothing is outside of his control. In this sense, nothing is outside of his will. Even the evil things that people do are part of his will.

When the early church first faced persecution

they prayed: 'Herod and Pontius Pilate met together with the Gentiles and the people of Israel in this city to conspire against your holy servant Jesus, whom you anointed.' (Acts 4:27) They saw a parallel between their persecution and the conspiracy to kill Jesus. And yet the church continued in their prayer: 'They did what your power and will had decided beforehand should happen.' (Acts 4:28) Murdering your Creator is not just an evil act; it's the epitome of evil! Yet the church said this is what God's 'will had decided beforehand should happen.' So even the sins people commit are part of God's will in this sense.

We don't know what God's sovereign will is ahead of time. But we always know God's sovereign will when anything happens because everything that happens is part of his sovereign will! He is working 'all things … for the good of those who love him' (Rom. 8:28). In this sense, God has a plan for your life, though you can only see it in the rear view mirror of life. It is a plan that encompasses every step you take and it is a plan that ends in glory.

This is a great comfort when we make decisions. It means that, whether we make good decisions or bad decisions, God's purpose for us is sure. And his purpose is to lead us home to glory. However much you might mess things up, if you are a true believer, then God will keep you to the end and the end is glory.

God's moral will

Second, the Bible talks about God's moral will. Some things please God and some things displease God. Loving your neighbour is part of God's moral will. Murdering your neighbour is not part of his will. God's moral will in this sense is universal. It's not specific to me.

'The secret things belong to the LORD our God,' says Moses in Deuteronomy 29:29, 'but the things revealed belong to us and to our children forever, that we may follow all the words of this law.' In other words, God's sovereign will is a mystery. Even when events unfold, we often find it hard to trace God's purpose in those events because 'the secret things belong to the LORD our God.' But God has revealed his moral will to us and he's revealed it in his word. Working out God's moral will is not a mysterious process. We just need to read our Bibles.

For example, 1 Thessalonians 5:16-18 says: 'Be joyful always, pray continually, give thanks in all circumstances, for this is God's will for you in Christ Jesus.' Do you want to know God's will for you? Here it is: rejoice, pray, give thanks. It's not complicated. It may not always be easy to implement, but knowing God's moral will is straight-forward—just read your Bible.

God's specific will?

What the Bible never talks about is what we might call a person-specific will of God. By a specific will I mean the idea that God has determined things I should do that are not also things other Christians should do in the same circumstances. It's God's will for me that I should love my wife. But then that's his will for every husband. It's part of his moral will revealed in Scripture.

What God has *not* done is create a plan for my life which I must try to follow that involves living in particular places and doing particular roles at different stages—a kind of timeline of things I'm supposed to choose at different moments. He doesn't have a specific will that I somehow need to second guess if I want to stay on track.

I moved to Boroughbridge in North Yorkshire in 2015. Moving to Boroughbridge was clearly part of his *sovereign* will, because here I am. Moving to Boroughbridge is not part of his *moral* will since it's not required of every Christian, otherwise every obedient Christian would be here! It is God's moral will that we should serve his people *somewhere* and Boroughbridge is as good a place as any. But it's *not* the case that God had a plan for my life that included coming to Boroughbridge which I had to discern and then choose to follow. In 2015, when my wife and I were deciding whether to stay in Sheffield or move to Boroughbridge, it was not the case that one of those options was God's will and the other was not. God did not have a plan for my life in this sense that involved moving to Boroughbridge. We could have stayed in Sheffield and still been obedient to God.

'The way many Christians practice seeking God's will before they make a decision,' suggest Mark Dever, 'amounts to spiritual and emotional bondage.' We are bound to live in obedience to God's *revealed* will, but on other matters we are free. 'I do believe that God's Spirit will sometimes lead us subjectively,' he says. He goes on to give an example from his own life when he felt God's leading. But, he says, he was free to follow that lead or to ignore it because it was not something explicitly mandated by Scripture. 'I could be wrong about that supposition. Scripture is *never* wrong.' He concludes:

> Most decisions I've made in my Christian life, I've made with no such sense of subjective leading. Maybe some would say that this is a mark of my spiritual immaturity. I understand this to be the way a redeemed child of God normally lives in this fallen world before the fullness of the Kingdom comes, Christ returns, and immediate, constant, unbroken fellowship with God is re-

established. A subjective sense of leading—when we've asked for it (as in James 1:5 we ask for wisdom) and when God freely gives it—is wonderful. The desire for such a subjective sense of leading, however, is too often, in contemporary evangelical piety, binding our brothers and sisters in Christ, paralyzing them from enjoying the good choices that God may provide, and causing them to wait wrongly before acting.[1]

Consider this. The Bible has a huge amount to say about *wisdom*. All of that teaching on wisdom would be redundant if every decision was zapped down to us from heaven. If direct divine guidance was the norm then the Bible would simply tell us to wait for a message from God. But a message from God is *not* the norm. When the Bible talks about waiting on God it refers to trusting him to deliver us rather than hanging around for a decision to be communicated direct from heaven. Instead the Bible equips us to make wise decisions. We're free to use our God-given brains to make wise decisions as long as the options are godly, our motives are pure, the gospel is our priority and the Christian community is taken into account.

I suspect some people cling to the idea that God constantly communicates which step we should take next because they want a sense of living in relationship with the living God. That is clearly a good desire. But it is such a *narrow* view of our relationship with God. God is interacting with our lives in a thousand ways every day. In his providence the Father organises our lives for our good. As we read the Bible, Christ speaks words of comfort and challenge to us in the power of the Spirit. The Father hears and answers our prayers. The Spirit is giving new desires and power to live holy lives. The Father generously provides for our needs. Jesus is present with us in adversity. Everyday the Holy Trinity is giving us joy, peace, comfort, forgiveness and much more.

God's guidance

We can do the same exercise with the language of 'guidance.' The Bible often talks about God guiding his people, especially in connection with Israel's time in the wilderness. God led his people in the wilderness through the pillars of cloud and fire. In the prophets and then again in the New Testament the exodus and the journey to the promised land is used as a picture of a new exodus. God has liberated us from sin and death through Jesus, the ultimate Passover Lamb. Now God is leading his people by his Spirit as we travel like pilgrims through this world heading for our ultimate home in the creation.

'The rising sun will come to us from heaven,' says Zechariah as he anticipates the coming of Jesus, 'to guide our feet into the path of peace' (Luke 1:78-79). Jesus is 'the way and the truth and the life' (John 14:6). He himself is the route we must follow. So the language of God guiding his people is used of his sovereign purposes in salvation.

The language of God's guidance is also used of his moral will. God guides us *to* his moral will and *through* his moral will.

> Good and upright is the LORD;
> therefore he instructs sinners in
>   his ways.
> He guides the humble in what is
>   right
> and teaches them his way.
> All the ways of the LORD are
>   loving and faithful
> toward those who keep the
>   demands of his covenant.

PSALM 25:8-10

Here is a promise that God will guide the humble, those willing to submit to the direction he provides. But notice that this guidance involves learning 'his ways.' That is, the characteristic ways in which God works so that our attitudes will mirror his attitudes (Genesis 18:19). And guidance is not a mysterious process. What we should do is revealed in 'the demands of his covenant.' 'Let the discerning get guidance,' says Proverbs 1:5. It's a reference to the wisdom found in the book of Proverbs. Or in Proverbs 11:3 we read, 'The integrity of the upright guides them, but the unfaithful are destroyed by their duplicity.' Integrity is a willingness to do the right thing. When we face tough choices, a commitment to obeying God's moral will is what ensures we follow the right path.

How does God guide? Through the Bible.

But what about ...?

At this point a number of verses or ideas might be clamouring in your head that seem to support the notion that God has a person-specific will for each of us. You may be saying, 'But what about …?' So let's look at a sample.

What about Gideon putting out his fleece? Surely, you might be saying, the story of Gideon gives us a mandate to look to God for a sign.

No. Gideon was *not* a faith-filled man who put out his fleece in an act of deep spirituality. Gideon was a *faithless* man who was hoping for a way out. He didn't need help making a decision because God had clearly told him what to do. God tells Gideon: 'Go in the strength you have and save Israel out of Midian's hand. Am I not sending you?' (Judges 6:14). That's pretty clear and God checks to make sure Gideon has got the message by adding the words, 'Am I not sending you?' Gideon asks for a fleece *after* this command. He put out a fleece because he *lacked* faith. The point of the story is that God can use even faithless, fearful people like Gideon. But don't follow his example and look for a sign. For, as Jesus said, 'Do not put the Lord your God to the test' (Matthew 4:7).

'Trust in the LORD with all your heart and lean not on your own understanding,' says Proverbs 3:5-6, 'in all your ways acknowledge him, and he will make your paths straight.' Surely this means, you might be thinking, we shouldn't make decisions for ourselves, but instead let God guide us. If we make our decisions for ourselves then our paths will be wonky.

No. We've got to read it in context. This section starts, 'My son, do not forget my teaching, but keep my commands in your heart.' (Proverbs 3:1) This is about trusting what God has taught and commanded in Scripture—his moral will. Your paths will be straight if you obey God's word.

Let's look at another example. 'Whether you turn to the right or to the left,' says Isaiah 30:21, 'your ears will hear a voice behind you, saying, "This is the way; walk in it."' Surely this means God has a plan for our lives and when we come to a fork in the road God will speak to us to tell us which way to turn.

No. Again we've got to read this verse in context. The very next words are: 'Then you will defile your idols' (30:32). That's the message people will hear in their ears. God says he will send 'the bread of adversity and the water of affliction' on his people so they turn from their idols (30:20). He's talking about his *moral* will revealed in the second commandment (Exodus 20:4-6). The voice they hear is the voice of Scripture reinforced by their consciences and the guidance they receive is God's moral will.

'"For I know the plans I have for you," declares the LORD,' in Jeremiah 29:11, '"plans to prosper you and not to harm you, plans to give you hope and a future."' Surely this means God has a plan for my life?

No. Again, we must read this verse in context. God is not talking to an individual. He's talking to his people as a whole and he's promising that they'll return from exile in Babylon. He's not saying, 'I've got a plan for you which you need to choose to follow.' This plan is going to happen *despite* their unbelief and disobedience. This is part of God's sovereign will to redeem his people.

What about a sense of calling?

What about a sense of calling? Surely the Bible talks about people receiving a specific sense of calling that God places on their lives?

But that is not how the New Testament normally uses the language of calling. It's true that Old Testament prophets often had a call experience in which they encountered God. It's true that Jesus 'called' the twelve to him to be his apostles (Mark 3:13) and that God called Paul to be an apostle (Romans 1:1). But none of us are foundational prophets or apostles of the church! We shouldn't expect God to appear in a glorious way (what's called 'a theophany') every time we make a decision.

The New Testament normally talks about 'calling' in three (somewhat overlapping) ways:

The call to faith and repentance comes to every person

First, there's a call to faith and repentance. Jesus, for example, says, 'I have not come to call the righteous, but sinners' (Mark 2:17). But this is not person-specific! This is the call that goes to *everyone* to turn and follow Christ. It's not some specific call to you alone. It's a call to everyone (see also Matthew 22:14; Romans 1:5).

The call to salvation comes to every Christian

Second, there's a call to salvation. 'Those [God] predestined, he also called; those he called, he also justified; those he justified, he also glorified,' says Paul in Romans 8:30. God has predestined or chosen who his people will be. And when those people hear the gospel, they hear the words of a person talking, but they also hear in those words the voice of the Good Shepherd and so they respond. This call comes in the power of the Spirit. The Spirit opens our eyes and warms our hearts and so we respond to the preaching of the word. As a result, this call is always an effectual call in the sense that all who hear it come to Christ. Again, this is the call that *every* Christian receives—see also Acts 2:38-39; Romans 9:25-26; 1 Corinthians 1:26; Galatians 1:16; Ephesians 1:18; 4:1; 1 Thessalonians 2:12; 2 Thessalonians 1:11; 1 Timothy 6:12; 2 Timothy 1:9; 2 Peter 1:10; Jude 1.

The call to holiness comes to every Christian

Third, there's a call to holiness. 'God did not call us to be impure, but to live a holy life,' says Paul in 1 Thessalonians 4:7. What's God's calling on your life? To be holy. But again, this is not person-specific. It's not any different from anyone else in your circumstances—see also Galatians 5:13; 2 Thessalonians 2:13-14; 1 Peter 2:20-21.

This is how the New Testament normally speaks about 'calling.' There's a call to faith. 'I have not come to call the righteous, but sinners,' says Jesus in Mark 2:17. But that call goes to everyone. There's a call to salvation. 'Those [God] predestined, he also called' (Romans 8:30). That's an effectual call because it comes in the power of the Spirit. And there's a call to holiness. 'God did not call us to be impure, but to live a holy life' (1 Thessalonians 4:7). But none of these are person-specific. These calls come to every person or every believer.

Called to be holy whoever, whatever and wherever

Or consider what Paul says in 1 Corinthians 7:17: 'Each one should retain the place in life that the Lord assigned to him and to which God has called him.' If you read that on its own then you might think Paul is saying every individual gets their own distinctive calling from God. And in one sense that's right. But that calling is not a quasi-mystical experience involving some kind of message from God. Look at what Paul says in context:

[17]Nevertheless, each one should retain the place in

life that the Lord assigned to him and to which God has called him. This is the rule I lay down in all the churches. [18]Was a man already circumcised when he was called? He should not become uncircumcised. Was a man uncircumcised when he was called? He should not be circumcised. [19]Circumcision is nothing and uncircumcision is nothing. Keeping God's commands is what counts. [20]Each one should remain in the situation which he was in when God called him. [21]Were you a slave when you were called? Don't let it trouble you—although if you can gain your freedom, do so. [22]For he who was a slave when he was called by the Lord is the Lord's freedman; similarly, he who was a free man when he was called is Christ's slave. [23]You were bought at a price; do not become slaves of men. [24]Brothers, each man, as responsible to God, should remain in the situation God called him to.

1 CORINTHIANS 7:17-24

Your calling is whatever situation you were in when God called you to be a Christian. The phrase 'when God called you' is a reference to the effectual call to salvation—in other words, when you became a Christian. Your calling is simply the circumstances of your life.

So your calling is not some special message from God to change direction. It's *the exact opposite* of that. Twice in verses 20 and 24 Paul says: 'Each one should remain in the situation they were in when God called them.'

- If you're a slave, that's the situation in which you're called to serve God.
- If you're free, that's the situation in which you're called to serve God.
- If you're a builder, that's the situation in which you're called to serve God.
- If you're an administrator, that's the situation in which you're called to serve God.
- If you're a mother, that's the situation in which you're called to serve God.
- If you're a husband, that's the situation in which you're called to serve God.

You are free to change those circumstances if you want (as long as you do so within God's moral will). Paul tells slaves, 'if you can gain your freedom, do so' (1 Corinthians 7:21). The point is not that you can never change your circumstances, but that *you don't have to* in order to serve God. You don't have to stop being a builder and become a pastor. You don't have to stop being a mother and become an evangelist.

Nor do you need to wait for guidance from God. You just need to get on serving God where you are now.

This doesn't mean God *never* intervenes to change the direction of a person's life. An intervention from God—a kind of direct divine steer —*can* happen. Some of you may have stories about when that has happened in your life. That's great and I have no desire to rubbish those experiences. After all, there are plenty of biblical examples. Philip is told by an angel to go where he will meet the Ethiopian eunuch in Acts 8. Peter has a trance in which he sees vision that sends him to preach to the Gentiles in Acts 10. Paul has a dream in which a man begs him to preach in Europe in Acts 16. Clearly God sometimes intervenes and sends people off in another direction.

But *this is not normal, nor is it necessary*. In each of those cases, Philip, Peter and Paul *were not looking for guidance* in this way. This is key. It came out of the blue. If God clearly directs you then that's great—we should be open to this. But don't look for it, demand it, expect it or wait for it. Get on with your life. Make decisions. Take initiatives. Go for it.

Go for it

That's the real message: Go for it. This is a *liberating* truth. Action can replace inaction. Initiative can replace angst. You don't need to wait around for some message from heaven. You don't need to be worrying that you're somehow missing the mark. You already have enough of a mandate in the Bible. So go for it.

Sometimes people tell me, 'I don't know what my calling is.' Here's what Martin Luther said to that: 'How is it possible that you are not called? You have always been in some state or station; you have always been a husband or wife, or boy or girl, or servant.'[2] In other words, your calling is not mysterious or difficult to discern. It's the current circumstances of your life. There's not some mysterious word from God waiting for you to discover. God has made his will clear in the Bible. Don't wait for a word; obey the word you have. Serve Christ in your current context.

I have often heard Christians speak of how a sense of specific call has sustained them when times have been hard. I can see how helpful that might be. But we are a people who are called to serve Christ through sacrificial love, costly service and self-denial. That is the call—the call to holiness and obedience that all Christians receive—that sustains us in tough times; that and the promise of Christ's presence, the Spirit's power and eternal reward.

I suspect that sometimes the real issue is that being a mother or an office worker or a Sunday school teacher is not glamorous enough. People want to be special and so they want some special calling. We all have a tendency to want to feel special and so we want a special call just for us. It's not enough to be called to be holy, I want something unique to me.

Well, here's your calling. I can tell you what it is with complete confidence. You're called to be holy whoever you are, whatever your role, wherever God has placed you.

We want to know who we should marry. So we come to God's word for guidance. And what do we discover? We should marry a fellow believer. 'Oh, come on,' we say, 'that's not enough. I want a name. At least give me a hair colour!' But as you read God's word you realise that what really matters is not *who* you marry, but *what* kind of husband or wife you are. Here's God's will for your life: that you love your wife as Christ loved the church; that you submit to your husband as the church submits to Christ (Ephesians 5:22-27). Or what you discover from God's word is that your life is not on hold if you're single. Your goal in life is not to work out who you should marry—you don't need to pick daisy petals or catch bouquets. By all means, get married if the opportunity arises. But in the meantime, here is God's will for your life: to enjoy him, trust him and serve him as a single person with the particular opportunities that singleness brings (1 Corinthians 7:25-28).

Or we want to know whether we should change our job. So we come to God's word for guidance. And what do we discover? God's will for your life is that you should 'obey your earthly masters in everything… with sincerity of heart… as working for the Lord' (Colossians 3:22-23). It turns out that, while *we're* interested in what job we do, *God* is interested in what kind of worker we are.

Decisions still have to be made and we'll consider how we should make godly decisions. But you don't need to worry that you've somehow failed to discern God's guidance and now the person you married, the job you accepted, the house you chose, have placed you outside God's will. Instead, what matters is that you are a loving spouse, a godly worker and a good neighbour. Go for it.

REFLECTION

1. Here are two statements that I read or heard recently. Are these appropriate things to say? What might be meant by them?

- "Can we pray for Owen as he considers where he may be being called? We would love him to join us here, but God may be guiding him somewhere else."

- "Father, we pray for Clare as she seeks your will. May she find your direction for her life."

2. How should we pray for someone:

- deciding whether to join a church planting team?
- deciding whether to marry to a particular person?
- deciding whether to look for a new job or accept a job offer?

2

DECISION-MAKING AND THE FAMILY
OF THE CHURCH

Let me tell you a story. It's a story (that I will tell with an enormous dollop of artistic licence) which begins with a French mercenary called René. René was bugged by a problem. How could he be sure that he existed? That anything existed? That God existed? 'René,' people said, 'what are you on about? Look at the world. There it is! You can see it, smell it, touch it.' 'Taste it,' they said (after all, they were French). 'But how can I know that what I see is real?' replied René. 'I'll show you how real it,' said a friend and promptly kicked René in the shins. 'Did you feel that?' 'I think I did,' said René in a pained voice. 'But maybe it's all just a dream.'

After that they left René on his own. 'I must doubt everything,' he said. 'No evidence is reliable – it might all be part of the Matrix.' Actually he didn't say that because he hadn't seen *The Matrix*. He said something along the lines of, 'Anything I see or hear might be part of the dream, the delusion. Doubt is all I have.'

But then René had a break-through. 'Maybe doubt is enough,' he said to himself. 'The very fact that I have this doubt must mean that I exist.' At this point he suddenly switched into Latin and declared, '*Cogito ergo sum*' which means, 'I think therefore I am.'

That moment would change the whole of the Western world. His full name was René Descartes and we call the impact of Descartes' argument 'the Cartesian revolution.' It was turning inwards.

Turning inwards

Here are two key features of the way that turning inwards continues to shape our culture. First, *what decides what is true is human reason*. The action takes place in my head; not in the world around me. Human reason is sovereign. Everything else, including the Bible, is judged by human reason. This why we have scholars reading the Bible and saying, 'This miracle couldn't have happened.' 'That story is probably not authentic.' Instead of evaluating human thought in the light of divine revelation, now in Western culture we evaluate the Bible in the light of human reason. Truth is decided by our minds.

Second, *what decides what is true is me on my own.* I can't trust tradition. I can't trust other people. I myself must make the decision. I'm on my own. Anyone reading the Bible would say, 'We love therefore we are.' Or, even better, 'We're loved therefore we are.' We are who we are as part of God's people, made in God's image, made to live in relationship with one another and with God. This is what gives us our identity. But René Descartes didn't say, 'We love therefore we are.' He didn't even say, '*We* think therefore we are.' No, you're on your own.

A lot is at stake. 'I think therefore I am' also means 'I am what I think.' Who you are—your identity—is now for you and you alone to determine.

That attitude has become deeply embedded in western culture. The western world is now extremely individualistic. Decisions that would once have been made in the family—that still are made in the family elsewhere in the world—are now made by individuals on their own. Parents wouldn't dream of 'interfering' in their children's lives. Teenage rebellion has become a rite of passage. Every since the 1960s we've seen a shift away from the biblical virtues of self-control and self-denial. Instead self-expression and self-fulfilment are the new virtues in our culture. Personal freedom is the value that trumps every other value (even the right to life of an unborn child). 'I decide how I will live my life, and no-one else has a right to interfere.'

But this attitude is also embedded in our churches. Our culture says, 'What decides what is true is me on my own.' And Christians, too, assume they will make decisions for themselves on their own. 'I decide how I will live my life, and no-one else has a right to interfere.'

And the emphasis is on what I feel. Our culture says that truth is decided in our minds and so we have turned inwards for direction. And Christians, too, turn inwards. I assume guidance takes place inside my head. I do what *I* feel God is calling me to do.

What happens in practice is that we co-opt God to back up our private decision-making process. 'I feel God's leading …' 'God has told me …' 'I have a sense of inner peace …' No-one else is allowed to have a say if I feel this is what God wants. God becomes a kind of trump card to protect my private, self-centred decision-making process.

Turning outwards

But now let me tell you another story.

Created in God's image for community

THIS STORY STARTS NOT with a man, but with God. God is Trinity. He is a community of persons. The Father, Son and Spirit live in eternal love. Our God is not a force running through the universe, nor is he a solitary being. He is relational. The persons of the Trinity are defined by their relationships. The Father is the Father because he has a Son. The Son is a Son because he has a Father. Father and Son are united through the Spirit. Three persons with a common being, a common love and a common will.

Once upon a time God made humanity in his image for relationships. We are human through relationships. Our culture often implies that we find our identity as we distinguish ourselves from others by accentuating our independence or difference. But we are made in the image of the triune God to find identity through relationships. You can no more have a relation-less person than you can have a motherless child. To be a child is *by definition* to have a mother. To be a person is *by definition* to have relationships

The account of the creation of humanity reflects this. Genesis 1:26-27 says: 'Then God said, "Let us make man in our image, in our likeness..." So God created man in his own image, in the image of God he created him; male and female he created them.'

The plural pronoun 'Let *us* make man' suggests a God who is plural and communal. God creates through his Word and now that Word is addressed to himself. And we are made in the image of the communal God. The God who said '*Let us*' makes us relational beings. We're people in community. He did not make us solitary. We are made *male and female*. We're made to exist in community and we're made for community with God. The trinitarian community graciously extends its communal life. We were made for community.

We were made for community with God. But after the rebellion of the Fall, Adam and Eve hide themselves from God. They can no longer walk with God in the garden. They're expelled from his presence. There's enmity between God and humanity.

And we were made for community with one another. But now Adam and Eve hide themselves from one another as they cover their nakedness. There's enmity between the man and the woman. In Genesis 4 we again see this conflict between people writ large as Cain kills his brother Abel.

We are still made in God's image. We want relationships. We still love and we still yearn to be loved. We still live in families and we still build community. But God's image in us is now twisted by our sin. Our selfishness corrodes relationships.

Families and community are vulnerable. Sometimes our communal identity can be tyrannical as one person dominates a family or an elite dominate a culture. Sometimes we deny our communal identity, opting instead for fragmentation. We choose to live as autonomous individuals.

Recreated in God's image to be God's people

INTO THIS MESS, God comes to Abraham and makes a promise: he promises a people who know God. It's this promise which drives the story of redemption. God repeatedly tells Abraham that his offspring will be as numerous as the sand on the seashore and as numerous as the stars in the night sky. Abraham will become a family and his family will become a nation. His name is changed from Abram to Abraham which means 'father of many'. Central to the purpose of God are not *ad hoc* individuals, but a community.

The promise to Abraham is not just the promise of a people, but a people *who know God*, a people among whom God is present (Genesis 21:22; 26:24, 28-29; 28:15). The blessing is not just to be a people, but to be a people who are right with God, a justified people (Genesis 15:6).

When we get to the book of Exodus we find the promise of a people has in some ways been fulfilled.

'The Israelites were fruitful and multiplied greatly and became exceedingly numerous, so that the land was filled with them' (Exodus 1:7). The family has become a nation. But they are a slave community. They are not free and, in particular, they are not free to worship to God. So God promises to liberate his people. At the heart of God's purposes is the promise: 'I will take you as my own people, and I will be your God' (Exodus 6:7). They're not only redeemed *from* slavery; they are also redeemed *to* be God's people. This promise that 'I will be their God and they will my people' runs all the way through the Bible story.

In 1 Kings 4:20 the writer says: 'The people of Judah and Israel were as numerous as the sand on the seashore; they ate, they drank and they were happy'. This is the language of the promise to Abraham (Genesis 22:17; 32:12). But this highpoint in the fulfilment of the promise is short lived. In 1 Kings 12 the nation of Israel is divided. Solomon's son, Rehoboam, oppresses the people until Jeroboam leads a revolt. The nation divides, becoming a northern and a southern kingdom. The sin of the people eventually leads to exile.

But God promises a new covenant. '"This is the covenant that I will make with the house of Israel after that time," declares the LORD. "I will put my law in their minds and write it on their hearts. I will

be their God, and they will be my people."'
(Jeremiah 31:33) Through this new covenant God
will fulfil the promise: 'I will be their God and they
will be my people.'

Recreated in God's image to be God's people through the cross and resurrection

THIS STORY REACHES it climax in Jesus. Jesus is both
God with us and God's faithful people. So he brings
both God and humanity together. 'There is ... one
mediator between God and men, the man Christ
Jesus.' (1 Timothy 2:5) As a result, Jesus is creating a
new people who know God. We're reconciled to God
through the cross and resurrection. We're adopted
into God's family with God himself as our Father.

And we're also reconciled to one another. The
cross breaks down the dividing walls of hostility
between humanity, uniting us into one new family
(Ephesians 2). The cross humbles us, stripping away
our pretensions and rivalries. The cross makes us
family. 'Because there is one loaf,' says 1 Corinthians
10:17, 'we, who are many, are one body, for we all
partake of the one loaf.' The cross wins our love and
defines our love. It reorients us away from self and
towards one another (1 John 4:7-13).

The climax of the story is a new humanity, people

from every nation gathered together around the throne of the Lamb, reconciled to God and reconciled to one another. At the heart of John's wonderful vision of the new creation is the fulfilment of the promise made through Moses: 'They will be his people, and God himself will be with them and be their God' (Revelation 21:3).

A renewed identity: we are family

THIS STORY, which is *your* story if you're a Christian, creates a very different way of thinking about our identity. It's hard for us to grasp how different it is because we're so immersed in Western individualism.

In the West the question 'Who am I?' has become one for which I am encouraged to find or create an answer for myself. So the world is full of people trying to earn their identity or prove their worth. As a result we lack assurance, or we lack contentment, or we put others down to bolster our own self-perception, or we are dependent on the approval of others, or we are self-righteous, or we are vulnerable to any circumstance that prevents us fulfilling our ministry.

But the key defining relationship for a Christian is our relationship to God. Who am I? I am a child of

God, the bride of his Son and the dwelling-place of his Spirit. And this identity is given to me by grace.

Becoming a Christian means I belong to God and I belong to my brothers and sisters. 'In Christ,' says Romans 12:5, 'we, though many, form one body, and each member belongs to all the others.' It's very striking language. We belong to one another. We own one another. We're responsible for one another. It's not that I belong to God and then make a decision to join a local church. I'm saved when by faith I become part of the people for whom Christ died. My being 'in Christ' means being 'in Christ *with* those others who are in Christ.' This is my identity. This is *our* identity. The loyalties of the new community supersede even the loyalties of biology (Matthew 10:34-37; Mark 3:31-35; Luke 11:27-28).

What are the implications of this communal identity for our decision-making? It means *we should involve the Christian community in decision-making to the extent that our decisions affect the community*.

Not top-down heavy shepherding

Please don't misunderstand me. This doesn't mean that the community or its leaders tell people what to do in their personal lives. Sometimes people use the term 'heavy shepherding' to describe church cultures in which the leaders direct the details of the lives of their members. The church becomes like a cult. It creates a dangerous context in which abuse can all too easily thrive. By its very nature 'heavy shepherding' is abusive and it can lead to other forms of abuse.

But the problem with heavy shepherding is not that decisions are made in community. The real problem is, first, that the leaders sees themselves as the personification of the community. They equate the community with themselves. So if you reject their advice then you're rejecting the community. The result is hierarchical and autocratic community. Biblical community is *not* about leaders controlling people. In fact the decision-making community needs to be a 360 degree reality. It needs to *begin* with the leaders. More than anyone, they should model involving the community in their decision-making. Leaders are to be culture-shapers and you shape a culture by modelling it rather than by imposing it.

The second problem with heavy shepherding is that the goal of Christian community is growing maturity. Christian leaders are important. But look at how Paul describes their role in Ephesians 4:11-14:

[11]It was he [the Lord Jesus Christ] who gave some to be apostles, some to be prophets, some to be evangelists, and some to be pastors and teachers, [12]to prepare God's people for works of service, so

that the body of Christ may be built up [13]until we all reach unity in the faith and in the knowledge of the Son of God and become mature, attaining to the whole measure of the fullness of Christ. [14]Then we will no longer be infants, tossed back and forth by the waves, and blown here and there by every wind of teaching and by the cunning and craftiness of men in their deceitful scheming.

The role of leaders is not to make decisions for us. Their task is to equip us and their aim is maturity. This maturity is something a community attains together. Our community life as Christ's body is to increasingly reflect our Head, Jesus. We become a community in which more and more people contribute to decision-making discussions as we 'speak the truth in love' to one another (Ephesians 4:15).

We make decisions for young children because they're not old enough to make good decisions for themselves. But as our children grow up we give them more responsibility. We let them make mistakes. We want them to grow in their maturity. Heavy-shepherding keeps people immature. Church members are infantilised by their leaders. If someone always makes decisions for you, then you'll never grow in wisdom.

Sometimes people come to me for advice and I

refuse to give it because I sense they want to avoid taking responsibility. They just want someone to tell them what to do. So I tell them, 'Think it through for yourself.' My aim is maturity.

This, though, doesn't mean you outgrow making decisions in community. You can't say, 'I've been a Christian a long time so I don't need to make decisions in community.' It's quite the opposite. A key sign of maturity is growing commitment *towards* life in community. It's true that one good reason for making decisions in community is that the community is a source of wise advice and so you might, to some extent, outgrow the need for that. But that's *not the main reason* for making decisions in community. The main reason is that our identity as Christians is communal. You don't *grow out* of life in community; you *grow into* it, otherwise you're not growing as a Christian.

Making decisions in community

If communal decision-making doesn't mean always being told what to do, what then does it mean? Let me suggest it involves two things:

- Making decisions with regard to the implications for our Christian community.
- Making significant decisions in

consultation with members of our
Christian community.

A single person typically makes decisions without regard to anyone else. Suppose you're single man and someone asks you out for a drink after work. You can make that decision without having to think about anyone else. No-one else is affected by that decision. No-one is waiting for you to come home.

But what happens when you get married? Marriage changes your identity and your behaviour needs to catch up with that new identity. Again, suppose someone asks you out for a drink after work. What happens next? If you're thinking as a married man then you'll think about the implications for your new wife. Will she be expecting you to come home? Will she need your help? Will she have other plans? You've got to think through the implications of your decision for her. In fact, thinking about it, it would probably best if you give her a call to check it's OK.

Your new identity as a married man means a new approach to decision-making. Your identity has changed so you can't make decisions on your own any more.

- You need to make decisions with regard to the implications for your family.
- You need to make significant decisions in consultation with your family.

It's the same for a Christian. Becoming a Christian means a new identity. You're part of a new family and that family is now your primary allegiance. The family doesn't makes decisions *for* us. But we do make decisions *with* our family and in the light of our membership of the family.

This will affect how we make decisions about money, work, schooling, spending, housing, time, holidays and relationships. It might include, for example:

- Discussing schooling to ensure maximum missional impact.
- Seeking advice on issues like courtship or conflict at work.
- Co-ordinating holidays to ensure continuity for an outreach project or to avoid clashes with church events.
- Discussing whether to pursue promotion when this might reduce involvement in your church and its mission.
- Identifying hobbies which people can be

involved in together to increase
opportunities to do evangelism together.
- Sharing family budgets and giving to the
gospel to ensure accountability.

Suppose you're offered a new job. You should think through what it will mean for your church family. Will a longer commute impact your time for community? Will the extra salary bridge a funding need? Does the new role create opportunities to partner with other church members to witness in the workplace?

Or suppose you're planning a holiday. You should think through how your absence will affect the church family. Is the church planning a special event at that time? Will enough people be around that week? Could you invite someone else in the church to join you—a single person or a needy family, perhaps?

This doesn't mean you need to discuss every decision with everyone in the church. Much of the time it simply means thinking through the implications for your church community when you make decisions. Often your small group will be a good context to discuss decisions you so you can hear the community's perspective. In other circumstances, it may be better to talk to one of your leaders.

I realise this means giving up control and everything in our culture tells us that's a bad thing because personal freedom has become one of our ultimate values. But God's word says: 'Do not conform any longer to the pattern of this world, but be transformed by the renewing of your mind. Then you will be able to test and approve what God's will is—his good, pleasing and perfect will.' (Romans 12:2) Are you going to be *con*-formed to this world or *trans*-formed by the gospel?

And think positively about what you're doing. You're no longer on your own. You're part of a family—a family that loves you and cares for you. It's a safe place to be. It's certainly safer than being left to your own devices. Yes, it's an imperfect family. But it's also a family filled with the Spirit of God speaking the word of God. Perhaps the real question is: Do you believe that?

We all want a place where we belong, where people know us, where people care for us, where we feel at home. The church is that place. Don't stand at the edge on the fringe. Come into the community and make it yours.

Advice for leaders

Begin by modelling communal decision-making. Go to your Christian community with decisions that you need to make. Don't expect people to do what you're not willing to do yourself. Emphasise that you're not simply seeking their opinions, but you want them to be part of the decision-making because it affects them as your church family.

If you're the leader of a small group then a discussion about a decision that someone needs to make is a great opportunity to teach gospel priorities. So it's important to shape that discussion. We're not simply trading opinions. Nor are we undertaking some kind of democratic exercise in which the majority view prevails, or a marketing exercise in which the reactions of a focus group are gauged. The criteria that matter are:

- How does God's word inform this decision?
- How does godly wisdom inform this decision?
- How do the priorities of mission inform this decision?
- How does this decision affect the Christian community?
- What are the heart motives that are shaping this decision?

People may come to leaders for advice because they're fearful of taking responsibility for their decisions. Such people need to be handled differently from someone who is self-willed or indifferent to the impact of their actions on the community. Sometimes people need to be challenged to make a choice for themselves.

We also need to be clear about the grounds upon which we counsel people. We may need to distinguish between the advice of a friend (which people can take or leave) and the commands of God's word (to which people must submit). It's important that people don't confuse these two! Sometimes it's helpful to emphasise both the parameters the gospel provides for a choice *and* the freedom open to someone within those parameters.

Our aim as leaders is to 'present everyone fully mature in Christ' (Colossians 1:28). A person will not grow to maturity if other people are making decisions for them. Immature Christians may well need help in making godly decisions. But the aim is that they grow through the process. It's often more important to focus on a person's heart motives than the options open to them.

∿

Reflection

1. What experience do you have of making decisions in community? When has this worked well? When has it not worked well?

2. What are the dangers of making decisions in community? How can they be avoided?

3. Think of a decision you made recently (or a decision you are facing at the moment). How will your decision impact your church community? How did you take the church community into account as you made the decision? How was the church community involved in your decision making?

3

DECISION-MAKING AND THE PRIORITIES OF THE GOSPEL

We've seen the way the Bible speaks of God's sovereign will (everything that happens is part of his plan) and moral will (his definition of good and bad), but not a person-specific will for our lives which we must somehow second guess. We've seen, too, the importance of recognising our communal identity as we make decisions.

But what do we actually do when we need to make a choice? What happens next? What are the nuts and bolts of making godly decision-making? Let me outline the key criteria we should use. They're also the criteria we should use when helping one another make decisions in the Christian community.

1. Gospel priorities

We don't need to seek God's sovereign will—that's what's going to happen whatever we choose or don't choose. Indeed, we *can't* know God's sovereign will ahead of time. Moreover, God's sovereign will encompasses our bad decisions as well as our good decisions. That doesn't mean our bad decisions are good decisions, only that God graciously uses them in his purposes. All of this means God's sovereign will is not *directly* relevant to which option you choose. Nevertheless, it's comforting to know that, what whatever happens, God's purposes are sure. You can relax. Your decision-making process doesn't need to be filled with angst.

God's moral will on the other hand *is* relevant. It's the *most* relevant factor in any decision. So the first thing to do is always to consider what the Bible says about the options before you. Your conscience, too, may come into play at this point. If a particular option makes you uneasy that may be your conscience flagging up to you that this is a wrong thing to do. Be aware, though, that our consciences can be misaligned. Paul says a person's conscience can become 'seared as with a hot iron' (1 Timothy 4:2). If we ignore our conscience enough times it can stop working properly. It becomes like scarred skin that's no longer sensitive. So we need to be constantly realigning our conscience by paying attention to its voice and by hearing God's word preached.

Suppose you're fed up in your current job and there's a vacancy for a role in a neighbouring town. Should you go for it? The first question to ask if whether this job is moral. If it's dealing illegal drugs then clearly it's contrary to God's moral will and that would be a wrong decision. But, obviously, most jobs are within God's moral will. Nevertheless there are other aspects of his moral will that you'll want to consider:

- It's God's moral will that you provide for your family's physical needs. Will this job help you do that?
- It's God's moral will that you nurture your family's spiritual health. Will this job help you do that?
- It's God's moral will that you serve your church family. Will this job help you do that?
- It's God's moral will that you proclaim Christ's name. Will this job help you do that?
- It's God's moral will that love your neighbours. Will this job help you do that?
- It's God's moral will that you give

generously to support gospel work. Will
this job help you do that?

Some of these may be competing factors so it becomes something of a judgment call. But these are the criteria that matter. The key thing is that your life is shaped by gospel priorities.

Often Christians make life choices by deciding first on the lifestyle they want. Except that in reality this isn't really a conscious decision. Instead, our assumptions about an appropriate lifestyle are shaped by the values of the world around us. As a result we pursue a lifestyle that's similar to everyone else. We live in the same sort of places, enjoy the same sort of holidays, drive the same sort of cars, and so on. Even if we can't afford the full package, this is what we aspire to. We worry about young people in our churches being corrupted by the values of the world, but Jim Wallis points out that the real problem is not that they have *failed* to learn our values; the real problem is that they *have* learned them: 'They can see beneath our social and religious platitudes to what we care about most. Our great cultural message comes through loud and clear: it is an affluent lifestyle that counts for success and happiness.'[1]

So it's all too easy for our decision-making to be driven by worldly values. The world around us assumes that wealth, power and status are the priorities that should shape our decisions and we are influenced by this. Like our friends and neighbourhoods, we aspire to a good education, a lovely house, a pleasant neighbourhood, an advancing career. We then overlay these middle-class values with a veneer of respectable Christianity. Don Carson says, 'There are Christians who formally espouse the historic faith but whose heartbeat is for more and more of this world's goods, whose dreams are not for heaven and for the glory of God, but for success, financial independence, a bigger house, a finer car.'[2] None of these things are wrong in themselves. But they're not to be our priorities.

Our priorities are to be serving the Christian family, caring for the poor, proclaiming Christ's name, reaching the lost. Often these priorities will overlap with education or career. We might may well have opportunities to serve others using our education or through our career. But whenever we have to choose, we will chose gospel priorities. 'Do not conform any longer to the pattern of this world,' says Romans 12:2, 'but be transformed by the renewing of your mind. Then you will be able to test and approve what God's will is—his good, pleasing and perfect will.'

But too often Christians aim for a lifestyle that is like that of the world around. To fund the lifestyle to which we aspire, we look for a job that best enables us to pursue it. With the job in place, we look for a home nearby. Only then do we look for a church and perhaps volunteer for some aspect of Christian ministry in our spare time. We might call this 'leftover discipleship.' My church service comes from the leftovers of my life and my Christian giving is from the leftovers of my money.

It doesn't have to be this way. We can flip this process into reverse. Instead of making our first decisions about lifestyle and job, we can make our church and its mission our number one priority. We begin with a commitment to seek first God's kingdom (Matthew 6:33). We stop thinking 'job, home, church, ministry' in that order. We turn the priorities of the world upside down. We start by seeing ourselves as members of God's family. Then together we think through our mission. This helps identify our personal role. Then we think about a home near our church that helps us contribute to its ministry. That might involve relocating to serve the needs of a local neighbourhood or to be close to a particular Christian community. Only then do we make decisions about a job and that choice is largely determined by what will enable us to do our ministries. Some might pursue a ministry through their careers, but they'll be intentional about that, seeing it as their way to serve Jesus, and not as an end in itself.

I recognise that life is more complicated and our choices are often more limited. A neat sequence like the one described above will rarely be possible. The point is to ensure our priorities are shaped by the gospel. Then, instead of leftover service, we will have 'whole life' discipleship. We will be content with whatever standard of living allows us to serve God and seek first his kingdom.

2. Gospel wisdom

The Bible has a lot to say about 'wisdom' and nowhere more so than in the book of Proverbs. The book of Proverbs repeatedly traces the link between actions and their consequences to help us understand the likely outcome of different courses of action. Wisdom is being able to make decisions with a realistic assessment of their consequences. So Proverbs often involve:

- Consequences: These often come in the form of 'Don't this "for" or "because" this is what happens." For example, 'Do not join those who drink too much wine or gorge themselves on meat, for drunkards and gluttons become poor, and drowsiness clothes them in rags' (Proverbs 23:20-21).

- Comparison: These often come in the form of 'better this than that.' For example, 'Better a meal of vegetables where there is love than a fattened calf with hatred' (Proverbs 15:17).

- Observation: These often come without moral comment, but necessarily prepare for us for the vagaries of life in a fallen world. For example, 'A bribe is a charm to the one who gives it; wherever he turns, he succeeds' (17:8). It is not commending bribery! It is preparing us to navigate a fallen world in which bribery often works (at least in the short run).

The book of Proverbs is not intended to be an exclusive repository of wisdom. It is full of wise advice. But it also models a wise way of looking at life. You, too, can observe consequences and make comparisons. You can use your observations on life to gain wisdom.

This is because Proverbs reflects a particular way of looking at the world. It assumes we lived in a created order. 'By wisdom,' says Proverbs 3:19, 'the LORD laid the earth's foundations, by understanding he set the heavens in place.' As a result there's order in the world. Humanity's sin has disordered or messed up God's world so the picture is now muddled. But there's still order in the world. God is still in control. 'The world is not driven about by erratic, arbitrary and accidental forces, but is maintained and directed by the order which Yahweh established at creation.'[3]

This is why there are predictable relationships between acts and consequences. This is what makes observations on life a worthwhile pursuit. Because of the order in creation, there are predictable consequences that follow from certain actions. In Proverbs, wisdom is the skill of living in accordance with God's order. 'Because the order of life is God's order, living in harmony with it is wisdom and righteousness.'[4]

Consider, for example, Proverbs 24:30-34:

I went past the field of the sluggard, past the vineyard of the man who lacks judgment; [31] thorns had come up everywhere, the ground was covered with weeds, and the stone wall was in ruins. [32] I applied my heart to what I observed and learned a lesson from what I saw: [33] A little sleep, a little slumber, a little folding of the hands to rest — [34] and poverty will come on you like a bandit and scarcity like an armed man.

Here are some consequences that the wise person can observe: most of the time a lazy person doesn't prosper. You don't actually need the Bible to tell you this, the wise person can see it for themselves. But, because human beings are often not very wise, the Bible draws our attention to it. It passes on the wisdom the writer of Proverbs has learnt from observation.

All of this is given to us in God's word so we learn to apply wisdom when we make decisions. There's a danger of other-spiritualising decisions. God has given us minds to think through the choices we have to make. And he's placed us in an ordered world where consequences can, at least to some extent, be predicted

God has also given us the Christian community which is full of wisdom. I wonder if you've ever thought of it like this, but your local church is full of specialists. If I want advice on my car I ask one of the mechanics in our church. If I want advice on my home I ask one of the builders in our church. If I want advice on my health I ask one of the doctors in our church.

In particular God has given older people within the church. We might call them specialists in life! They have experience and wisdom which they have accumulated over many years of being a worker, a spouse, a parent. They may have learnt how to cope with illness, prosperity, redundancy, bereavement. They've walked with God for many years.

So Paul instructs Titus to exhort older women to disciple younger women (Titus 2:3-5). Paul himself describes Titus as 'my true son' (Titus 1:4). Here is Paul as an older man nurturing the faith of the young Titus. Paul is giving us a picture of a community in which older men and older women teach younger people, and in which younger people are seeking out the advice of older people. This is profoundly counter-cultural. Our culture is obsessed with youth and in which the young define what is important. In the process we've lost respect for older people. Old people have become irrelevant, even a problem. We've lost a willingness to be fathered or mothered. We've lost a desire to be guided and shaped by an older person. Think about this. If you call someone 'old' or 'old man' you're being rude. It might be a joke, but the joke only works because 'old' is bad in our culture. This is not normal! This is not how it's been in the past. This is not how it is in most of the world. Yet according to Proverbs 16:31, 'Grey hair is a crown of splendour.'

Look to apply wisdom when you make decisions and look for that wisdom in the Christian community.

3. Gospel motives

But true wisdom goes even deeper. 'The fear of the LORD is the beginning of knowledge,' says Proverbs 1:7, 'but fools despise wisdom and discipline.'

We like to think of ourselves as rational beings making rational decisions. But the reality is our reason is shaped by our hearts. *We find reasons for doing what we want to do.*

There's not necessarily anything wrong with this when the desires of our hearts are pure. The problem is our reasoning process is often corrupted by our sinful hearts. We all too easily 'rationalise' impure desires. We do what we want and then find reasons to justify our choices.

So true wisdom and wise decision-making begins with the fear of the LORD. It begins with a recognition of the holy God who knows the secrets of people's hearts. It begins by aligning and re-aligning our hearts to God's will.

Again, this is why we need the Christian community. Because we so readily find reasons for doing what we want to do, we need one another to help us see when our reasoning is corrupted by our sinful hearts.

Can we get real? I've been a pastor for 25 years. In my experience, often when people feel they are hearing God's voice or receiving his direction they're actually hearing their own desires. This is one of the big problems with the turn inwards that, we have seen, is a central feature of the modern world. We turn inwards, expecting to hear God's voice, but what we actually hear are our own desires. And often they are selfish, proud, sinful desires.

As student I used to pray each day with a Christian musician. On at least three occasions he claimed God had told him that God was going to give an expensive piece of musical kit. On each occasion nothing materialised. Here's one explanation of this. God made a promise which he failed to deliver. I hope you realise that can't be true! For the living God is unfailingly faithful to his promises. He always has the power to deliver and he must be true to his word. It's not just that he doesn't lie; he *cannot* lie. So I began to realise something else was going on. My friend was interpreting his own desires as God's voice. When he turned inward he heard his own desires, but then chose to interpret them as God's voice.

It's the same with a sign. If you look for a sign to confirm what you have already decided you want, then one way or another you will find something to do the job. Consider Rachel. A number of people warned her not to begin a relationship with an unbeliever. She ignored them. Instead, when one person said it was a good idea, she took that as confirmation from God. She claimed to be reading God's direction from the circumstances of her life, but all she was hearing was the echo of her own desires.

Or consider John. When John got a visa to go to Malawi he took it as a sign that this was God's will for his life. When his church leaders questioned whether he was the right person for the role, he told them how disappointed he was at their inability to recognise God's direction. Perhaps going to Malawi was a great option for John. But it may be that John is looking for anything to confirm his desire to go and ignoring good reasons why he shouldn't go.

Suppose you start a new venture in your church, perhaps a youth club or debt advice service. Soon, though, you face hostility from local people, tensions within the team and a funding crisis. Is this God telling you that this was a wrong direction, that he has other plans for you? Or is this Satanic opposition, a sign that, if you persevere, this venture will lead to much fruit? I've heard both explanations given for difficulties. Clearly, in his sovereign will God uses circumstances to shape our lives. But it's hard for us to interpret our circumstances; more often than not we can find reasons in our circumstances for doing what in our heart of hearts we want to do.

Or consider that sense of inner peace which is so

important to the way many Christians make decisions. Suppose I face a choice between a horrible job and a pleasant job. Suppose I turn inward and discover a sense of inner peace when I contemplate the pleasant job. That's not necessarily divine guidance! That's just a natural response to the choice I prefer. I'm hearing an echo of my own desires.

That's a benign example. But what if the choice is between joining a church plant in a poor neighbourhood or an established church in the suburbs. Again I turn inward and discover a sense of inner peace when I contemplate the suburban church. Again, all I may be hearing is an echo of my own desires, only this time they are selfish desires. We take soundings from our hearts, forgetting that 'the heart is deceitful above all things and beyond cure' (Jeremiah 17:9).

What if the choice is between continuing in a difficult marriage or bailing out in favour of another partner? I turn inward and discover a sense of inner peace when I imagine my wonderful new life without any of the strain of my current marriage. Is that God's guidance? No, it's a horrible echo of my sinful desires. The point is our feelings are not a reliable guide.

A few years ago a friend told me how a pastoral post in a northern England post-industrial city received no applicants. Meanwhile a similar post in a wealthy town in the southern English home counties received over 40 applicants. Does God call more people to serve in comfortable locations? Maybe. But I think it's more likely that people's sense of guidance is actually an echo of their own desires. I don't mind if you want to live in the home countries. But let's be honest and recognise that, despite all the spiritual-sounding language with which we dress up our decisions, most of the time we choose to do what we want to do.

And there's nothing wrong with that! It's fine to choose to do what you want to do—it would perverse to do otherwise. It's only fine as long as we're examining our motives to ensure they are gospel motives. We need to ask ourselves, 'What's really driving this decision?'

How can we do this when our hearts are deceitful and self-justifying? The answer is simple: instead of turning inwards, we *turn outwards*. We turn to God's word and we turn to God's people. We turn to people who will question our selfish desires. We need the challenge of other Christians.

I often have the opposite problem. I'm so suspicious of my own desires that I can end up reasoning that whatever is the worst option must be the right option. Or I can think that just because I want something it must be the wrong option. By God's grace, I'm part of a group of fellow church leaders who have met together regularly for over twenty years. On more than one occasion they've had to tell me not to be so ridiculous!

Remember we're not looking for God to zap the decision down to us. We're not 'seeking his direction' or 'trying to discern his will' because, as we've seen, the Bible doesn't speak of a person-specific will of God as the norm. So our aim is not to distinguish God's voice from our own desires. We're free to make decisions for ourselves. But those decisions need to be shaped gospel priorities and that means our hearts need to be shaped by gospel motives. True wisdom is to live for God, in the fear of God.

Let's review where we've got to by considering how we might define a good decision. A good decision is:

- a decision within God's moral revealed in the Bible
- a decision shaped by gospel priorities
- a decision that considers the implications for God's people
- a decision informed by gospel wisdom
- a decision driven by gospel motives

4. Gospel grace

So there's a freedom for us as we make decisions. It's not that God has one decision in mind for us and we need to second-guess what that might be.

But we can still make bad decisions. A bad decision is a decision outside of God's moral will revealed in the Bible, or which is not shaped by gospel priorities or not informed by gospel wisdom or not driven by gospel motives. And we may have to live with the consequences of our bad decisions. We can mess things up.

But even when we make bad decisions, God is in control. His sovereign will is sure. He will use everything that happens to us to make us more like Jesus and he will lead us home to glory (Romans 8:28-30).

And God is gracious.

On the night Jesus was betrayed the Apostle Peter made some bad decisions. In fact, he made the same bad decision three times (John 18:15-18, 25-27). He chose to deny his Lord. After the third time Jesus looked at Peter, and Peter remembered that Jesus has predicted this is what would happen (Luke 22:56-62). Then Peter was filled with remorse. 'And he went outside and wept bitterly,' Luke 22:62 tells us. Perhaps he thought he might never be able to serve

Jesus again, certainly not as a leader. Perhaps he even feared his relationship with Jesus was over.

But God was gracious. The risen Christ came to Peter and three times asked him, 'Do you love me?' It's interesting that Jesus goes behind the decision itself and behind the priorities it reflected to explore Peter's underlying motives. 'Do you love me?' That's the thing that really counts. That's the compass that will set the direction of our lives.

Then three times Jesus reinstates Peter with the words, 'Feed my lambs... Take care of my sheep... Feed my sheep.' (John 21:15-17) Peter made a bad decision. But there was grace and therefore there was a future for him.

You may have made bad decisions that continue to affect your life. You may, for example, be locked into a big mortgage that limits your ability to serve Christ. You now need to work long hours to cover the costs or you unable move to join a new church plant. You may have made that decision because you were driven by worldly priorities or accepted unwise advice or were driven selfish motives.

Or you may have made bad decisions about a relationship. Perhaps you feel like you married the wrong person or your marriage has ended in divorce. Perhaps you were unwise. Perhaps you chose appearance over godliness. Perhaps your priorities were worldly and your motives were selfish.

You may have to live with the consequences of your bad decisions, perhaps even for the rest of your life.

But God is gracious. Your relationship with Christ is as a strong as ever, for he will not let you go. And you can still serve Christ. In his sovereign will God has placed you where you are now. He's given you a role only you can perform. This is your calling. You still have a future. You can still be fruitful. The final words of Jesus to Peter was simply this: 'Follow me! ... You must follow me' (John 21:19, 22). And this is his word to us. Whoever, whatever and wherever you find yourself, follow him.

Reflection

1. Think back to a big decision you made recently: where to live, what to do with your money, what church to go to, what ministry to focus on. Jot down the stages you went through in making that decision. What were your non-negotiables in decision-making—things that you were

unwilling to question? How many of those things were gospel-centred?

2. What is the difference between an ungodly decision and an unwise decision? Can you think of an example of both?

3. Can you think of an example when wrong motives clouded your ability to make a godly decision?

~

Further Reading

Garry Friesen, *Decision Making and the Will of God*, Multnomah Press.

Phillip Jensen and Tony Payne, *Guidance and the Voice of God*, Matthias Media.

Kevin DeYoung, *Just do Something: A Liberating Approach to Finding God's Will*, Moody Press.

4

A DECISION-MAKING CHECKLIST

Father God, I ask you to give me
the insight to understand your word,
the humility to submit to your people
and the wisdom to assess the options.
May my heart be undivided
in my love for Jesus
and my trust in your care.
Amen.

1. **God's will**: What does the Bible says about this issue?

Are the options within God's moral will?

. . .

2. **God's people**: How might each option affect my church family?

What is the view of my church family?

3. **Gospel priorities**: Which option will best enable me to serve Jesus?

Do any options reflect worldly priorities for wealth, status or power?

4. **Gospel wisdom**: What are the likely consequences of each option?

What is the advice of people with experience in this field?

5. **Gospel motives**: Is this decision shaped by love for Jesus and trust in God?

Are any options driven by fear, pride or selfishness?

Reflection

Consider the following scenarios. Answer the questions from the decision-making checklist. What would you do in each situation? What factors might make you change your decision?

Scenario #1

Harry has enjoyed getting to know Sharon and now he's wondering whether he should ask her to marry him. She's a member of his church and seems to be a godly young woman who is serious about serving Christ. She's from a working-class background, grew up in social housing and now works as a shop assistant in a local shoe shop. Harry was educated at a private school and, after graduating from university, has joined the family firm. Status is important to his parents and he's worried about how Sharon will fit in his family's social circles. Harry has also thought about serving as a missionary to unreached peoples whereas Sharon seems to have no desire to leave their home town.

Scenario #2

Colin and Anne have been attending the church in their village ever since they moved there five years ago. The congregation each Sunday is about 25-30 people. The church runs a toddler group and that has led to a number of evangelistic opportunities. It doesn't have a paid pastor, but the two men who lead the church are competent and committed. Colin and Anne's children are 13 and 11. They're worried that their children don't have anyone else their age within the church. So they are considering switching to join Cornerstone Christian Fellowship, a large church with a lively youth group in the nearby town about 15-minutes drive away.

Scenario #3

Wendy is married with two teenage children. She currently works in the HR department of a local company. The department is not well managed which often makes Wendy's working life frustrating. Next week she's got a second interview for a job. It's with a smaller company with just two people in the HR team. Wendy would be the team leader so the new role would be a promotion, with more pay and more responsibility. It would add 45 minutes each way to her commute and will probably mean longer hours. Most days she wouldn't arrive home until getting on for 7.00pm. Her husband says he's supportive though Wendy suspects he doesn't really want her to work longer hours.

∽

NOTES

1. Decision-Making and the Will of God

1. Mark Dever, 'The Bondage of "Guidance"', *Together for the Gospel*, February 20, 2008, http://www.t4g.org/2008/02/the-bondage-of-guidance.
2. Cited in Marc Kolden, 'Luther on Vocation,' *Word & World* 3/4, 1983, 386.

3. Decision-Making and the Priorities of the Gospel

1. Jim Wallis, *The Soul of Politics*, Fount, 1994, 137.
2. Don Carson, *The Gagging of God*, Apollos, 1996, 465.
3. Daniel Estes, *Hear, My Son: Teaching and Learning in Proverbs 1-9*, Apollos, 1997, 26.
4. Graeme Goldsworthy, *Bible Probe: Proverbs*, Scripture Union, 1981, 11.